Level 1 – Beginning
Short and simple sentences with familiar words or patterns for children who are beginning to understand how letters and sounds go together.

Level 2 – Emerging
Longer words and sentences with more complex language patterns for readers who are practicing common words and letter sounds.

Level 3 – Transitional
More developed language and vocabulary for readers who are becoming more independent.

abdopublishing.com

Published by Abdo Zoom, a division of ABDO, PO Box 398166, Minneapolis, Minnesota 55439. Copyright © 2019 by Abdo Consulting Group, Inc. International copyrights reserved in all countries. No part of this book may be reproduced in any form without written permission from the publisher. Dash!™ is a trademark and logo of Abdo Zoom.

Printed in the United States of America, North Mankato, Minnesota.
052018
092018

Photo Credits: Alamy, iStock, Shutterstock
Production Contributors: Kenny Abdo, Jennie Forsberg, Grace Hansen, John Hansen
Design Contributors: Dorothy Toth, Neil Klinepier

Library of Congress Control Number: 2017917511

Publisher's Cataloging in Publication Data
Names: Murray, Julie, author.
Title: Reptiles / by Julie Murray.
Description: Minneapolis, Minnesota : Abdo Zoom, 2019. | Series: Animal classes | Includes online resources and index.
Identifiers: ISBN 9781532123009 (lib.bdg.) | ISBN 9781532123986 (ebook) | ISBN 9781532124471 (Read-to-me ebook)
Subjects: LCSH: Reptiles--Juvenile literature. | Herpetology--Juvenile literature. |Speciation (Biology)--Juvenile literature. | Reptiles--Behavior--Juvenile literature.
Classification: DDC 597.9--dc23

Table of Contents

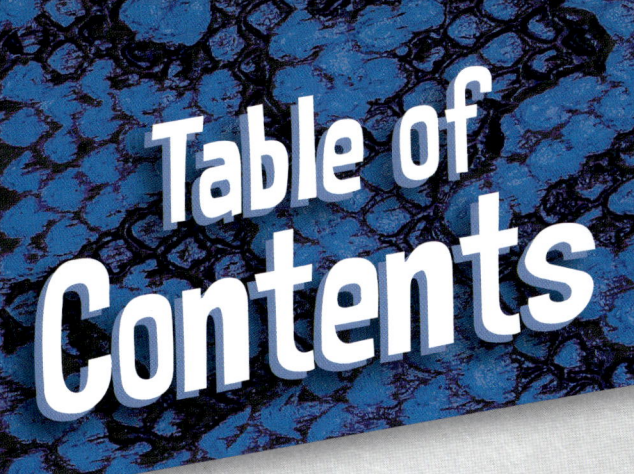

Reptiles 4

Reptile Traits 22

Glossary 23

Index 24

Online Resources 24

Reptiles

Reptiles live in many places. Gila monsters live in the desert.

Reptiles are **cold-blooded**. A horned lizard sits in the sun. This keeps it warm.

Reptiles are **vertebrates**. A crocodile has a long backbone.

Many reptiles have legs. Some do not. A milk snake slithers on the ground.

Reptiles have **scales**. Some have hard shells. These protect their bodies. A box turtle has a shell.

They **shed** their skin. Snakes shed their skin in one piece.

Most reptiles lay eggs. An alligator lays 20 to 50 eggs at a time.

A saltwater crocodile is the largest reptile. It can be 15 feet (4.5 m) long!

The smallest reptile is a leaf chameleon. It lives in Madagascar. It is just over one inch (25 mm) long.

Reptile Traits

- Are **cold-blooded**
- Have a backbone
- Have **scales** or **scutes**
- Some **shed** their skin as they grow
- Most lay eggs

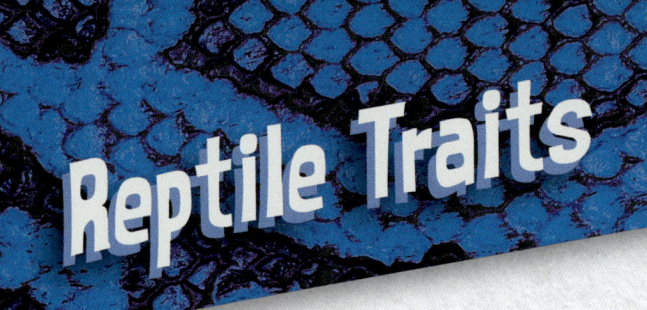

Glossary

cold-blooded – having a body temperature that varies with the environment.

scale – one of the many small, hard, thin plates that cover reptiles and some other animals.

scute – an external bony or horny plate or large scale that some reptiles have. A turtle's shell is covered in scutes.

shed – allow skin to come off to be replaced by another one that has grown underneath.

vertebrate – an animal that has a skeleton with a backbone inside its body.

Index

box turtle 13

cold-blooded 6

eggs 16

Gila monster 4

habitat 4

horned lizard 6

leaf chameleon 20

Madagascar 20

milk snake 10

saltwater crocodile 19

scales 13

shedding 15

shell 13

vertebrate 9

Online Resources

Booklinks
NONFICTION NETWORK
FREE! ONLINE NONFICTION RESOURCES

To learn more about reptiles, please visit **abdobooklinks.com**. These links are routinely monitored and updated to provide the most current information available.